FROM MIMIR'S HEAD

FROM MIMIR'S HEAD

poems from *theforestforthetrees*
(1994–2000)

Charles Stein

Station Hill
of Barrytown

Published by Station Hill Press, Inc., 120 Station Hill Road, Barrytown, NY 12507, as a project of the Institute for Publishing Arts, Inc., in Barrytown, New York, a not-for-profit, tax-exempt organization [501(c)(3)], supported in part by grants from the New York State Council on the Arts, a state agency.

Online catalog: www.stationhill.org
Email: publishers@stationhill.org

Design by Susan Quasha
Cover photograph by Charles Stein

Some of these poems were published in *Golden Handcuffs Review*, (editor: Lou Rowan), *Sulfur* (editor: Clayton Elshleman), and *Sunfish* (editor: Nigel Wood).

Library of Congress Cataloging-in-Publication Data
Stein, Charles, 1944-
 From Mimir's head : from theforestforthetrees (poems, 1994-2000) / Charles Stein.
     p. cm.
 "Some of these poems were originally published in Golden handcuffs review and Sulfur"—T.p. verso.
 ISBN 978-1-58177-123-7
 I. Title. II. Title: Poems, 1994-2000. III. Title: From theforestforthetrees (poems, 1994-2000). IV. Title: From the forest for the trees (poems, 1994-2000). V. Title: From Mimir's head : from the forest for the trees (poems, 1994-2000).
 PS3569.T363F76 2011
 811'.54—dc22

                                        2011023825

Printed in the United States of America

Contents

A Little Off Somewhere

The Hat Rack Tree

Your old hat sits
on the Hat Rack Tree

as the plumes
of the tree
grow dry
and wind unravels them.

"No wind
is the King's wind."

Now you go to buy some new
hat.
      Should it be
just like it?

A new hat sits like a plume
on the Hat Rack Tree.

There is a bird
on a lady's hat.

Would you pluck its felt
or shred the brittle veil
that hangs from the brim?

It is a crow
(not my crow).

Something not alive
on the Hat Rack Tree.

What can I do with this?
What can I sell?
Come all comers
to the Hat Rack Tree
and see the lady's hat with black stuffed crow!

Odd — but the crow's eye lives
with terrible rays
and the feathers shine
with a glint of green —

Wind in the branches
wind in the plumes

strong enough to knock your
hat off. Knock your hats off.

◆

If you were a King
and owned a tree

would you become a crow
with its terrible shining
and charm the wind
into your hat

and wear it
out
to see the world?

◆

A lady's veil
conveys her shining.

She is nervous.

Nor does she glean
the thing on her hat.

Here

is an idea.

Don't think it.

Don't think "here."

It's just a thought
that stops the mind
and gives it locus.

Apart from that idea
where is the mind?

It's just a word.
A bird
in your head
's bright warbling.

"Be Here Now."
Or else: "Off somewhere."
Your choice.

Where's that tree?

Not here.

Off somewhere.

Alone
in some blue mind.

Those visions
that came
in the hat you wore —

just put it on — and it
puts *you* on. That hat
you have
puts *you* on.

◆

Picasso came to your house
in secret.

He was a friend of the man who
beamed it up.

And now the only place there is
comes home to roost
as THIS place —

a courier of *Place Itself*
against all feeble *Heredom*.

◆

There was a bird
in some century

and certain women *now*

were it
then.

And they danced
         in place —

they danced the place —

in its very center
dancing.

                ◆

Take the thought of place away
and the things
in their shapeliness
take up space
into their very nature.

The shape it was
sat down inside it.

                ◆

Now a blot comes down. All light.
It passes through old walls
and takes our thoughts back.

666 Characters for Brad Keeney

On a certain bench
you sit with known companion
gazing at a shelf where nothing is.
No objects.

Poof: Out of that nothing
a little skull appears
carved by ancient peoples
—black skull and old.

Poof again: Out of nothing
a little cup appears,
a treasure of the Grandfathers.

Now the little hairs
rise on tense
necks. Eyes
bugle from shadowed sockets.

No law obtains.

A doll — dull black — with three long wiry strands
sprung from the spine
looks about to do a doll-dance,
does a doll-dance

causes sound
to bang against the brain

as if of dancing.

The Fan

Two hands
hold time.

Whose?

Old hands: new
blood pulses
through
old
hands.

I don't think a clock's hands,
but the odd old span itself.

A fan between two hands — one
an old hand, the other
ever-not-young-yet.

Are these two hands
one hand — held
in the far expanse
of time's blank fathoms?

Between these hands,
all the sounds time beats,
all vibration's colors, all the scenes.

The Sound of One Hand?
No sound. But a fan flashed

to show the scene
but hide the mind

behind the face
behind the hand.

◆

Now the fan is closed.
The mind itself
has turned from the scene.

How High The Moon

I want
to name
that spoon.

Is that what you are doing?

Or is there something else —
something elusive, illusory, allusive,
something just about to be known
but now not *yet* known

hung in the gallery
at night
when the snobs can't get at it
where the minds of others
with other things *on* their minds
have to hang back and keep their minds' hands off
that shifty thing
that shiny spoon.

Aren't you going to finish this poem?

No.

I can't conceive
the end I'll meet —
what move
my mind

will move
my hand
to make

      then
    now
       when some
new thought comes

what will it be like?
I dare to wonder

flashing from some un-
remunerated covert
of the mind
without precedence —
oblique to all association's linkages —
a new thought
dropped
or popped
from the oblivion
before it was …

Now some new bird thought
joins the swooping flock.

Now the bird flock
loses itself
behind the tangled boughs
of some mind's
trees.

How high
's my mind?

From what
does the moon
hang
        leaning
over
empty woods (or words)
to see the animals
scramble?

Some mind, stopped,
but whole. Like the full
moon's round
between the hyper-focus of the
        winter-branched
    black twig bush — as light
that doesn't
cause known things
to *be* known but
decimates as it allows
crows
to flourish
in the moon's flash.

Or else a certain light
of grain
blown against the dim
  sun's dust veils'
    golden aureole

and a ravaged mental state
so that the grim Plutonic brother

takes all definition back
with his woozy drumming.

"That's Poetry, boy!

"Do you *know*
        how *hard*
                it *is*
                to compose *Hex*ameters?"

                I'm broke.

My tooth is laid
        on the table by the spoon.

No more chomping stones
    between my thoughts:
I have to get up on the back of a pig
    and stand there too
    as it slogs about the yard muck
    snuzzling for a thing
    to sink its mindy snout in.

Aren't you going to finish this poem?

No.

A big wind.

And in the wind

wood, pigs

radios,   a lady's foot

a garrulous old fart
    that can't get a word in
edge-wise
                against the wind
the wind's so hard —

a huge hammer
and a mighty stone

roll in the heave …

Someone calls on the hotel phone to say

all the forms you filed have failed to say
the things the forms are filed for. Someone calls
on the hotel phone to say
the world you left for holiday
has vanished as *you* have
vanished, *out* of that world —

Someone calls on the phone to say
the Written Word's discredited,
the Spoken Word — and has it ever been?
They take your car away.

Someone on the phone has called only to say
the Old Hotel consumes the signs
by which the world is strung —
nothing but rooms
            surrounded by light —

This is how it is.
How it seems.
Seems for me.
How Being seems.

Some deep displacement
tussles with the norms —
dislodged, but not too far,
(not far enough
for abject force
to storm relief).

I think so.
A black hat on a white
table
        budges
on its own whim—

as if that. As if
the crockery jiggled
from some
        metaphysical
                impertinence, some
                principle askew, some
                        arguable
                        invariant
                        discredited
                                after all …

    At your very premise
    a hairline fracture
    rigs the whole.

    No thought remains.

    No law obtains.

    Bright sun is all.

"I will not enter the gate ..."

                                But

just as that thought's out

the portal turns about

and there you stand

across the perilous line.

Past Being's Thrall

Color's Being

in color
rests.

And thunder's?

In the ponderous hearts
of local weather gods.

So much for the structure
of being's categories.

That gods
are denied
by ponderous minds
forefends no thunder's menacing.

Whack! and the oak
is riven in the yard—

Then mind's alert
past being's thrall.

Three Lectures on Cosmogony

1

Of course
I'd like
to be an expert
on your gods

        (check out the sources
           reckon the losses).

According to me
even these
tribal peoples
mean what I say.

2

First there was

no number, therefore

no First

was. And

there was no   logic, therefore

no Therefore. Not even And.

Not even Not.

You could say anything.

3

Where does the meaning gather?

On an
other
side of
all of this?
turned away from us?
leering back at us?

And the jaguar, Studebaker, or whatever it was
that covers us
stalking us

　　　　—there
　　　　　　where meanings linger:

　　　　　　　　eyes of meaning's hunger

　　　　　　　　　　to devour the things

　　　　　　　　　　　　that meanings mean.

Crow's Head Run

1: "My Crow"

The roundness of the crow's
head
—the bigness
of the shining
well-appointed
head
of the large crow

sleek
and big
and with a head
of an
un-
speakable curvature—

about its earthly business
near the shadows
on the lawn

       itself of the nature of the shadow it bestrode
a hole
in space
moving
across the grass
in golden sunlight.

◆

Do meanings
singe
the things
that harbor them?

Do things
bring meanings
home
to port?

Do they carry
meanings
in the vessels of
their being here?

Do the colors
of the day
once awakened to
in the openness
of wonder
betray us to
our ancestors?

Imagine
a distance
as vast
as ancient
Chinese
wind gods are
apart from
matter's things
that made it into history—

that's how far
away

your meanings
seem.

◆

The meanings of the crow's
head

's curvature's
disquietude

black and shining.

◆

The accessibility of
the common world
removed] Well, it

never had been accessed, actually, had it,
by anyone, precisely. A blur
in reality. [Metaphor. Not blur, only.

Not just fudged   edge you could focus
better if you had the
HARDWARE—

The hand to grasp it sleazes off somehow. The in-
accessibility of the Real
is
essential TO
the Real. Making "accuracy"
a matter of style.

(People get nervous if you hold
the thought you've honed
UP TOO CLOSE
up in their face

             like:

the gesture
overwhelms
the coin.)

     ◆

What is the context for improvement?
Is the order type
of the continuum
"the world"? Or
some model
FOR the world. And are we free to vary
the rigor of the model
according to the use we choose?

     ◆

Rounded
head (or some such curvature)
and the colors
of the plumage—
as meanings
known, home

to sit black shape
on black naked branches—

And without there being a voice imparting knowledge and
without there being someone—anyone—

to send a message home to—
without a god
in the ancient sense
of storied verities—
only the business as you've put it together for yourself
with the makeshift equipment of a difragilating
noosphere—a language only
your own through use, not sourced
in own
source—
domesticated, not native
to the mind
the mind not native
to itself: domesticated, a little off somewhere

                                        [Quoth: the Dog

        ◆

Call the crow's head
"being" and the gliding movement
planing across the golden twilight of the lawn shadow
"time."

The crow
is outside
time

(the way its
head
bows or rotates on
the sleek
fat
neck

the feathers of its wings
tucked in in circumspection

its yellow eye

the visible shining of an information
essential to itself that
is not
seen.

2: "The Consequence of Crows"

Everything has
"vestments" save
let us call it the "the infra-mass" —everything
has form
but this.

Like something caught in the corner
of the eye—if you
fix your gaze
it vanishes, like the Pleiades.

And there are hollow stones (crow stones)
that rise from the infra-mass
so that it seems
to seem

a definite ground to all
our jagged sculptedness.

◆

Theory of vestments and investitures:
being
without a nature
covered

by points.

♦

     The blandishments of wildness and hair
growing from the fat lady's belly.

She is buried
under the pavement and when she heaves
the city undergoes
permutations of its ethnic hegemony.

♦

There is no authority
to the wilderness;

its utterance
cannot be affirmed;

therefore: no retrenchment
is feasible.

♦

Did the odor of the damaged
septic system
change
to that of the wafting of blossoms when
your concentration deepened on your breath

and the infra-matter
whose nature is as subtle as the color of the sky
confirmed itself—
(that's a *question*.)

◆

Mind's filaments

the veins and runnels underminding speech

speech under gesture

gesture ruling the bodily

"the rush of immediate transition"

white water
on which
intelligence
steadies itself
discovers itself

without haste—
no budging   no adjustment
no urgency
but the unimpeded urgency
of sustaining
an intractable mobility
without act
or designation

articulate
              in the interwork ...

Three Public Matters

A Manager's Song

in a boat
in the night

with a bird on the wind

above my own black waters ...

They take
my time
away.

    Getting the goods
from the point of manufacture
to the temporary storage depot
and out again to the point of distribution
without damage
        for small cost
            in a timely fashion —

The agitated mind examining the depots
        arranging for the passaging —
the checking operation, the detail
that cannot be ignored —
no slippage in the execution of detail —

The hideous activity of calculation
        never to be neglected;
the anxious fingers beating on the little number pads;
the angry conversations
        the anguished accusations
            the rejoinders

the null espousals
the ecstasies of rigorous calculation.

Pleasures in the errors of the adversary,
the errors of the competitor—
joy in the misadventures of the others—
the relishing of misfeasance
committed by the others
(at first to one's annoy, but later perceived in a new light
and deftly turned to advantage).

The sentiment that one is charged with the protection of one's own
and thus a dedication to heroic labors
—working into the night
through meals
without adequate rest or recreation
at expense of health
good cheer
affection of spouse and comrades
to the detriment of others
and one's own ...

in a boat
in the night

with a bird on the wind

above my own black waters ...

Prayer

*(Offered at the Festival Celebrating
the Return of the Seventeen Year Magico-Cicada,
June 1996, Kingston, New York)*

White noise   poised in miasmas
   among the atmospheres
of dying lilac
 and the rain
  of black walnut
         blossoms.

Your sound
  in swelling ranks and choruses
behind the morning birds
  behind the noon trucks
   behind yourselves.

Overwhelming
  ocean of voices,
   vast depot of messages.

If ever before
      then now—
If forever   before
      then   forever.

May the sounds in my head
    extend
      forefend
    defend
       upend
          surrender me.

May your judgments be pertinent
your surveillance, profound.

May the poisons
    and excisions
        of the human
        saturation of all habitat

not terminate the brood.

West Pittston

The day before he died
the FBI came down here.

They found sump'm.

He got so excited,
                he died.

Yuh understand what I'm talkin' about?

I know all the stuff was goin' on.

I shouldn't say nuthin' —
I saw the good he did,
I saw the bad.

How many slips did he give people?

When Peach died, he had all the records.

We wuz lucky.

The next day
        he was down to Jerry
                lookin' for a job.

Jerry's a powerful man—all the livings and all.
They feared him.

Sure, they fear'd him.
        He was J C—Jesus Christ.

During the flood,
    he ran all around tryin' to help people.
What'd he get?
So the money he made —
he had it comin' to him.

Jimmy?   Jimmy?

He wanted me to DO stuff.
I told him no —

Then he died
and his son went to jail.

That was his own fault.

But he didn't know
    half of what his father know'd.

Yeah, but he wasn't payin' attention —
he shoulda been payin' attention.

I was promised all this stuff
    and I didn't get nuthin'.

Nah — you wasn't promised nuthin' —

They lied like a rug.

Something from an Outside

First it was a panther   menacing my path
to the house in the woods an old friend guarded,
but soon it found its prey   small deer or other
woods beasts   though my terrified foot-fall retarded
approach to the door.

Then it was no such thing but a creature
I ought to have recognized from the story
we'd been told   FROM   OUT   OF   SPACE

composed of something matter proved
irresistant to
—its banana bunches and scythe-arching gestures
passed through the screens and glass
of all-protecting cabin walls.

A cult.   And now I think—THE cult—
the one that laces my ancestry—my father's
blood cult line song I met
one figure from in my Dark Retreat's last day's
dream—it was of Outside—"Not
a figment of the blood only"—though three
women wished me to be their partners
for the night or always—I felt that they as members of
the actual group or cult that I attended—they were there for real—
for all it was worth—possessed identities by being there. But for me
there was another matter in my concern that brought me
to these meetings and I felt the falseness
of my situation a hindrance to response.

I could fly, certainly—easily sustain
the mental concentration on the locus
to which I wished to elevate my body
and BE there BEFORE I discovered myself
to be there   projected by a will
I must anticipate and open to—passively receive.

These skills were noticed by the members
of the cult group and perhaps, it occurs to me now,
this was the sign they saw that I
was *of* them.

I wasn't *of* them—
for the secret they sought and saw
I held in the place in me they
took for being one with them—was
(and is this not the secret of all secrecy, all cultic mystery?)
knowledge of the *in*-existence of the very thing
that most they thought bestowed true being on them—that I saw
the empty canister where their research projected elixir—
and in that in-existence
traversed a different space
with a deeper if less gladsome luminosity.

But the *thing* we saw at the banister
with banana arms and alien almond eyes
was of a totally different ideo-ontology—not given
by the insight I already had attained. The acts
appropriate to its initiation of us
were neither in my repertoire nor theirs.
But *they* possessed a narrative
to align themselves upon its strange intent
—or so their practice eased them—
while I could barely urge myself
to remember the story at all.

Yet they (the creatures? the members?) had come to *me*
in my ignorance and emptiness.
And, I am now certain, will come again.

Megalith

It is not a natural thing to keep large stones
planted in the earth. No roots
commingle with the fundament.

Each is singularity; therefore, no law
modulates
relations with
environs. Rather
environment abounds within the stone.

The spaces
that obviate
density

are infinite
and luminous
with no source.

This is the place where physics
is raised an octave.

We are invited
to be
the stone
just where our own proclivities
discover emptiness.

Stone dons no mask
                    and yet
                            it

will not be dissuaded from the carnival.

The mind behind the head

doffs the head
and dons these trees
as the face it shines

dons this world of evening dwindling light
as if to speak by means of it

as if to hum its quiet colors lingering into silence

a face no more unless a face of night

a head whose darkest absence
is the ranging mind in it
thought in night itself
without a face

Once in dream speech

the other
kind-
's disabled

so that all speech is of the dream kind

and all of what speech speaks
and all of what it speaks of

's tinctured
dream.

◆

Here where
dream
speaks

the world's
a stone

and stone
compound
of light

and light
of speech.

The man

in the text
lies
on his back.

His face
is words.

He keeps silence

but causes sounds

to break out in your eyes.

From Mimir's Head

The Loons

We have been here forever.
              The dream
stops.   Or the words
that once were emergencies
gathering the mind
to a fine attention
pass from attention.

Relief. The anxious searching.
Where have they gone —
old words
taking us with them—

Arise and are gone,
the many white moons
scattered on the ripples—
        the loons
          like little lithe canoes
as the ripples
                ride them.

Now I can do anything.

The mountain-trembling thunder
   erupts behind the mulberry tree.

My mind can stop the world it legislates
 and then start up again, blue sylph
on water-fracture—tiny
   ripples over tiny stones.
                      Nobody
knows who I am. No
body knows
who I am.

How the rain dumps—
   effervescent water-froth—how the house lights flicker.

    ◆

Don't make too many distinctions—
   or make them all—
   go all the way—
the water from its sources
   broken into a thousand
   minuscule rivulets—

And when the waters join and distinction ceases—

   Walk away in the night, all power forgot.

All   the mules   have   walked away.

At least their *bodies* were mules.

Walking others' stuff up difficult passageways was
                              what these bodies *were*.
No matter how deep you look   you don't find matter raw.
                                          The mules' joints
if ugly—still they were fit to trudge. Trudging
mud. Mules. In midnight mountains.

If words say it—you can't judge
just because of that. Mud is shining mud is
red. It cakes, takes shape, breaks, baked into
bricks. If you build something out of a thing, don't curse it.
The sounds have revenge on a mind that superimposes
its own structures   over those the raw sounds have.

Nothing is just an animal, just mud.
The horrible smell of the newly dead,
the huge vitality of larvae swarming in the corpus—
"the dead elk
is full of night life."

All   the mules have walked away.
They *know* what you think.

The Power

to fat itself
on forgetting
the name of the horse goddess
leaping through the general conflagration
disguised as a person
tasking the international night
for a feast of dreams
and inside one of them
to find her—find the goddess
flare her nostrils
turn her head—
the night horse goddess
come out of a hole in the rock, her plumes aflame

Ogdoad

as you approach
the powers beyond
the Eight Powers placed by
the Demiurge
                    to become
one of the Powers yourself
    merging and emerging
in and from the sizzling
  day-night sky
                        best not forget
        the little dreams that
        nightly bite at you
        —that something has snipped
        your prick off and you are
            having a devil of a time trying
        to stick it
        back on
                        that your teeth
        with such furious
            efficacy have crunched
        down on themselves
        that now they crumble
            from your gums

    the condition of
    these conditions—
        these versions of
        an inner life coeval
        with each other—

        the crime and the ascension
            the ignominy and the *gloire*—

in what weird arena
    do we dream
        they stand as one?

Not   to deny   that something
sits in "shrubs" or "shrooms"
to prompt the speech of the stars if
the Possible   open it   if no bullying facticity
overrun the Possible   and if no fantasy exhaust it
in locationless expenditure. The cover of Time Magazine (June 17 1997)
presenting the inward strangulation of the
vertical almond-eyed aliens
that see but are not in the seeing   seen
whatever the judiciousness and humor of the journalism—
are here among us

looking through the pages for some hint of light

an emerald
     sitting on a purple pillow
   (how does the mind enthrone in an ambience?)
            a milky cloud above the ancient house
so that the green bauble *means*
         on its elegant purchase
   if it but ride
      a certain glance

     the text unread
       but *for* that glance
     among the paragraphs

      when what is there
   (there in the mind—there in the text)
  unseen, unknown,
        beyond phenomena

           leaps onto the world

The failure of the poets to imagine the world

the possibilities lie unclaimed
   in Mimir's head

at the bottom of the sea
the skulls' eyes teem
   with uncut minerals

it is impossible that the possible fail (of possibility)

but the phantoms that haunt the floating shells

the dead leading the dead
   to something less than mortuary slumber
by being somewhat more—

the barely audible thumping
   of the blocked   possible

   (my horoscope promises freedom from want—what
will they not
            take away?

                        never swim again in pristine waters
                              never drink again
               light over night hills

                        the little ripples passing on the lake
                              from the mountain bottom

If it doesn't bite
don't believe it's wolf teeth   gate   the god's speech

The Sampo

Two Greek words that specify
the mythic complex associated with Hermes:

κλεπτειν (kleptein): to thieve. But more primally:
to be in a certain state of magical excitation;

and

δολος (dolos), plural δολοι (doloi): wiles, guile.
What tricksters know.

At the primal site of the logos—Hermes, then.

At night

and far beyond ordinary deceitfulness
a state of moral intent
dangerous and full of
unanticipatable patterns of power.

That the business poets have conducted on mythic terrain

remain

the space of attention
a certain preoccupation with language
must return to.

Hermes
not
a pile of stones
only
but if border markers—

a registration of the unsortable basis of assortment—
all manageable order is provisional and
    in the manner of a "cap" or covering

      a basket
         tightly woven
       inverted over
           the sacred stump
        of the ruined
       axis
     tree
         whose pith
was a gateway
        to inundating
   waters
     of tribal
    cosmos
   mind
       dark and teeming.

   Had to put a cap   to the potent
                water-spout

    as in the dream cartoon the anxious
       animal has to put something—anything—atop
            the spouting spigot
but then the property of this capping device, this basket or
              whatever—
      just how the woven pattern lies—
        imposes itself as a condition of
     the further situation Jackal
    Man or Hermes Coyote has to
      improvise the consequent response to.

Poetry now
      had best take stock
      of the means
         of its own situation

on the ever-narrowing margins of a global socius
has inverted
      the ratio of means
    to mind's intent
         so that the waters
       themselves now seem to offer
     inalienable informations of order and the teeming
       feral darkness
           of magical induction
      goes unremarked

Something nervous at the end of the line.

The little chains of littler

shining droplets—the smallest spheres of the visible
filling everything
and being spherical
shining
with the information
of everything everything that can be known
crams itself into their evanescent chaining

you are a knot
and the knot has unraveled itself
and the cord
is made of the most intimate unimaginable kernels
of your nature
you have penetrated into a region of your own intelligence where
indifference to all
of what turns out to be the mere
combinatorial play of the informations stashed within the chains
is hot with the full measure of your care

you *care*

but you don't care about THAT—no prejudice regarding the outcome
or the onrush
of the specifications of the combinatory

all drawn up in a knot
and the knot dissolves—has already dissolved—has always dissolved

And without phenomena

Song

Cat on the porch
Hegel in the book
Urge in the belly
Bird in the wind

Barge in the bay
Train.

Weed in the ground
Worm in the blossom
Mind in the brain
Wind in space

Space in time
Truck.

Form.
Hat.

Cat looks up at me
with light-tightened eyes.

Words on the page
make report
of their own
event.

Crows in the light.

The Tower

The people talking
about their lives
and planning
actions
and reactions to the deeds
of others with opinions
formed or opinions
culled
and repeated
and circulated thus
so that these thoughts in circulation
encircle the lives that form them
and a tower goes up
on the outskirts of the village
to which everyone recurs—refers
with slant-long glances
down in the shadows of it

Heart Lake

Every   outward   ray
has
all along and thru
an inward, backward—

That nozzle
            focused on the plot
                        has
up its rope of shining gush
a backwards*
            toward the aperture

                        *[an attraction
                        drawing back
                        that is the force
                        that threw it forth—
                        the force that threw it   forth
                        attractive
                        all along the outward path]

—LIKE that—

the energy
opening the world   making the world   open   up—
Can and should and must and always is
met—as IF met—
by an energy closing down
releasing all strife and urgency—
open arms and falling
home to the abyss—
open arms and happy
just where struggle   taut and pressing hard
                                    toils
                                    goal.

71

Now, that "happy"
       is a delicate field
              insidious of fair color
passing through all circumstance
       without geometry—released, released
it radiates
              in undulations continuous
                     but of no source
     filling the indefinite contours, opening spaces.

              And how the heart is an opening hollow
                            in opening breast
                     and fields the emanations of all things—

◆

Where does all this rancor   come   up from   then?
How does it accede
       to its own form—
its accurate sprockets
       that clank each prong on prong
to sprockety object?

Tree stump sawed off after thunder struck,
obstructive metal face,
smooth office wall

       stop the sensitive fields
              abrupt the fielding

              Oh don't stop now!

An arm

     —arm and hammer—
thumping   making
         breaking

  urging toil and making brave
     to brave the abruptive noise of it
the slam and whack without neat interval
shattering all poise
         is
only the outward shot
     of an inward releasing—
something released in the gut
    let go
        no strain
that then the hammer slam
      to smash
       or join—

And yes the quiet
     settling of the pond water
  the vesperal disbursement of the perturbation of the breeze
so that the cross-current wavulets of surfaces, interfering,
quiets down
       to a smooth glaze

is only to give a sharpened hardness to the surface of tranquility—
            an edge that takes the breath away

  as moon blade stands over black shadow mountain

        doubled
          without disturbance
             on the pond.

CANTO

How can I live   before this inquiry
flushed through the body
resolves itself in light without remainder
and all detail
flicker betwixt an essence that imparts
itself by withholding itself and an absence that
withholds itself, imparting itself
and all is known and what
is known loses itself in what there is
to be known and what there is   to be known
cannot be known   unless it lose itself
in the body's luminous web-nets—the golden
edges of the water planes in sunlight above
the brown   bottom

the roundness of the poem's shape
cutting off all incredulity driving
the argument, forcing the interminable toiling
of cerebral energetics through the coils of a syllogistic
yet to be descried—the evasiveness of formal
decision on either term—the poem's
finality and the mind's
tragicomedic earnestness to cohere

And then went down in structures of proven
stability but dubious source
to the permutations of a shining sea—
its artifacts and adventures,
its islands of periphrasis, its tropical resource
And heard the rigorous
music that withholds itself

just beyond the ear of inquiry
so that the force that drives it
cannot be brought to court
and these interminable soundings
fill up the world phase

June Run 6/97

6/15/97

an impossible text.
Just try it. coming on like that.
A dictation   from an absentee
mindlord   leaving
his tracks
on the mindfields of his
strained amenuensis

♦

Without a camp
on money's
margins
    where number
dwindles
        into another
capacity of measure—

You cannot *critique* money, without
having a go at
the   *Mind* of money.

        (*The mind of money thinks a world* ... or: *only money*
explains money)

A Revolution
    through
        the Possible:

what IS
          issues the moment of Might Be—
     sustains it   proffers the Possible AS possible
NOT "it just might be possible" but

     Possible Because It Is

          the Voice
               will be *distracted*
               from its stance
                         just this amount:

you can hear the inward talking
                    but you are unnerved by it, don't
               know how to pick it up
                    or let it out
          of your problematical serenity
                              let it sound
               and respond   in kind.

Someone is walking outside the room
     tweaking the lighting.

When she decides to come in here
this poem is done.

6/16/97

We are only
pretending
    to write
        this poem. Beyond
      the scene
         another operation
     emanates causations.

The Crystal
         Palace packaged with
       "commodities" —[versus] packed
    in an in-
  con-
    spicuous

     dark
      wet
    mom and pop
          shop in some
      Creole district
    prof'ring rutabagas and other roots

    "people eat rocks and stones
      with the dirt left on them"

The aura
  of course
     has passed
   from the magically charged and
    enigmatical emblemality of an
  epoch
      long   gone by ("the pigs have won")

What have I left behind here?
Shall I go back
and pick it up?—
        go back
to the top of the page
and find the gaps
and fill them up
with thoughts I want to
propagate just now?

Ideas   bleed across stillness—silent, still themselves.

        Suddenly
a face lights up
in the center of a sunflower.

Suddenly a fact
lights up
as a mind alights
upon it—

            a butterfly
                floats down
                    on the bough.

6/17/97

At night
the mind
that wants
to sing
    brings
sleep along with it
            —sounds of plaster peeling from old walls
    find their way among the neural tissues.

People in this culture talk to God [or *the* god]
in tough situations. Ask:
Must I do this or that, that or not?
And give their reasons.
And God or *the* god replies
with a rattling of oak leaves
in the mind, that is,
in body's subtle waftings, torrents, lights,

Don't just drift: Cut!
And start up new—
the railroad train in the night
arriving, passing
down by the ancient river
also behaving like that—

Something else is always going on
beside the delirium

of commodities—the names
things suffer themselves
to be buoyed up by—

the woodchuck cannot conceive of it, nor can Midnight—
our cat Midnight
operates
in non-conceptual eruptions
elegant
without anticipation
in spite of the seemingly limited ensemble of behaviors,
                    to her species general—
She likes the scent of roses now abloom
    on the bush that merges   with *her* bush—and sits for hours
imbuing herself with their fumes.

What's the point?
        It's there—YOU find it. I
have other things to do with
what awakeness is left to me
than fish out and make explicit
the thematic of my images and instances
marked in words and phrases now gone by.

What for instance?

                Something oblique to commodity
        occult in the business of things—You go back there!

6/18/97

Tired enough
   and the language
   starts to tumble
           toss and bite
finally
       down on the meager eruptions
    twinkling in the brain
               down on concrete things:

       a cup
     on a desk's
         black blotter, a door key
      without memory
         placed by a dented
                 spoon

     the cup—Chinese
         with broken handle—broken off, that is
      it *has* no handle

A key to a door
I've opened before
       surely
          but now
I do not know
      what the key is for.

I wish I had that trove of ancient keys
I bought from Stan the day I also purchased
clock parts in a big jug   that tinkled
in a distinctive way   when I jiggled it

and Stan
from the back of the store
heard the little sound
and knew what it was.

The concrete
according to Karl Marx
is the result   of many
determinations.

If you know what just this something is—
if you can say it, if you can give
more and more detail about it

that is because the thing itself is the focus
of many histories—here
a lot of thinking   comes home to roost.

What it hatches
is
your mind—
its particular instances.

But the concrete is
a wonder too   the instance of a not-so-readily-
discriminable thaumaturgy.

Fall to the bottom
of just what comes to mind or comes to hand—go with your
attention—
don't change anything
don't try to know

anything
            allow just what wants to come up
        liberally to do so

Don't choose
            Don't solicit
                    Do not name

[try this as a counter methodology—another praxis to speculate the
                                                real]

only, on your part, be there, in your place
for whatever arises, with whatever determinations

and you will see, *pace* Marx, there are *none* ... no determinations.

        ◆

    the bastards.
Just that. The ratchets
        have *them*
            and so they'd
        ratchet
                    us. But *our* words
        urge
                away.

To another venue.

The Hermit

The Hermit

Is it not sufficient ecstasy
to live at the Rim,
to find oneself a watcher on
the labyrinthine passageways?

Inside the circle of fire, a black orb vanishing.

Without the fire, there is no fire.

The moon, a glass-orb'd goddess object.

◆

That change cannot befall
what already is only change —

there is another order under that —
the purchase of the Will.

◆

The Artifex is a lantern man
harnessing his fire
to focus force
and force the world to burn
according to his measure,
as moon is measured change.

That man   at the summit
             of the pointed peak
                  either seen or seeing
             is of the Rim —

shrouded, hooded, haloed
                                  by black light
           the vanishing orbs of that which the Rim encloses

           the labyrinthine manner of the passaging
                               between an absolute harnessing
                     and the Horse Itself.

It was a matter of the station of the image.
To say that the harness were the moon
or that which only, when the orb is full,
declares its cool hegemony
convening an order at the cost of freedom—
as if to budge and twitter, to flow and dance
to give gesture to being
without prevenient harnessing
were freedom—

Yet the time of dancing is the full of the moon
     and its ordered changes, figures
                                  dancing.

No interdiction of the Image will withstand
                               The Harnessed Horse.
There is a course
                     before the choice to curb its very flowing.

The business was to find it
                               and to interdict
           not Image but false ease—

to find the means by which apparencies
fold up in their possibility
to *be* apparencies—

their links with truth.

Every word a seed
the hazard
of a step
in a labyrinth—
accordingly, you cannot even know, while coursing, if it *is*
a course
if there is
a goddess object
nested in its midst—
a welcoming orb
gnoetic and refreshed
at the end of hazarding—

Every word an image
nested in a thought
every thought
harnessing its image
but giving it rein—
letting it run—
thought running with thought—

And the thought
is the labyrinth
that passes
between not *saying*
but *knowing*
Being

and a dark hegemony
that passes as light
and calls its goose-step
dancing.

◆

Horses
burning.

◆

There was a knowing
that set a course
of motion
to find the very thought
that set it out—
a motion toward the rim of an outstretched prairie:
West. A city
Of thought: East.

◆

The trace of the motion itself
confirms a text—
it shimmers   dissipates
dispels
its urge
of onset
renewed
at every site within it
since surely every station
is a word
and every seed
a coil

                                        wound and waiting
                        to hazard the moment
                                of its labyrinthine passaging—

The Self   back East: Jerusalem—
Was.   The City on the Hill
Is.

The thought of a certain rigor and
the thought of a certain height.

The Artifex, the Hermit, a tall
building. At night.
Or with night
inside it.

        An elevator shaft
core   shooting from nine sub-basements up
to the rotating tower, dizzy with starnight.

The building harbored a man—
an infinite call—a voiceless howling—
the rushing of the wind void
contained within the hollow
of the shaft
so that a core of tone emerged—
raspy, no longer voiceless,
a twine or chord of pitches
pithing the void.

That building *loved* us
in spite of its howling,
and we, at the bottom,
on the street or sidewalk
from which it heaved its enormous upness—
we were taken up into its sound—

     Laughable

          Outside of the world
             Outside of the void that funds it

    Unutterable

       Monstrosity

           Renewal

      The Promise

          Better than …

The Point of Names

The Point of the Point

there was no space before there was a point in it
and if there was a point
its radial expansion toward the sphere
was there
too

first there was something like a sphere

all the possibilities
nicely coiled in its rapture

the eyes of cats the shapes of worlds the vicious
cyclicities all
convened in that possibility
of possibility

its story now
echoes in this chamber

the point
of the point
of return

the inherent divisibility within
the undivided
the course
of space
in that which took place
nowhere—

time coiled in the ruby's asterism
the smoke snake going up from the gem of now
the nasty genie hovering
spoiling speech
from the site of its own unfolding

the snake that coils the world
the dignity
the menace

the fangs of aeonic monstrosity
the python winding the torso
of the human form asserting the form of the world—

Beyond the cracker thinkers and the characteristics
of which the wise seem so redolent

contracted inside the very measure of apparency
there is a measure
there is no measure

why is there always another commentary, another torment
turning the real?

the beauties of surface glittering hideous monstrous

the call to adjustment

the yearning for the more that is minimal and the small that o'er
                                           hurdles the tallest
reaches the light in the grim the spasm of satisfaction the itch
scratched
in the groin of extremity

from inside the cloud of too much of everything this itching looking
dark within for the path to simplicity once more

there
in the dawn wind
on the frosted window plate
where the sun strikes up ever glorious
as if the subsequent had never spoiled
as if there had never been a *day*
the spinning thing come round another time all new all over
the primordial spheroid a whirligig in nothing

the ever unreadable sociality and oblivion released
by the gestures of recall

Pineal Matters

Inside the marble
                bauble
                        bead or egg
        (spherical
                spherette
        pebble
                bubble
        bublet
                globule
        tigle seed or drop

 All the geometries
coil
        in the smoke snake
of the ruby's asterism

All the possible
                configurations of apparency
                        lie folded

        And the globule
                has a face
        it faces Up
        it looks Up, takes Light, knows Sky—

forget about it. The machine
got jiggled and the process went on "tilt"—
you couldn't see the sky anymore
    the possibilities
                        took *hold* of you

made of *you*

         a path among themselves

  very tiny, very stupid,
very self-concerned

and the globule
went blank, went black
  shriveled up

and the doctors examined it and declared
it had no function, no need to think about *that*— no need
to feed
the bauble
with the light it craved so bad
forget about it
they told everybody and they did, we did
forget about it

Until now — the
whirling of the light about
the meditating corpus
simultaneously both ways at once
the counter-rotation of the rings and cylinders
resonating with geometries
              forgotten
                until now, so
Transduce your care to another
chronotopy altogether the vectors
of appetite torque and spatiality grows mirthful—
spiring gyres co-merge and syrinx noises shoot into the one
panophony of rapture

  rupture
the catacombs of forgetfulness

break open
the decanters
of the sky

and sat down

right on top
 of the flat-
tened pyramid
and waited
for the surge ...

it came

and the grids
convened

and the loathing
ceased
and the lesion
closed
and the imperturbable bottom
advanced itself
in a ceremony
without ceremony
it was the end
 of every stiffness
the gestures
were full and luminous
and instructed our movements with accompanying sonorities
discerned by the open ear all eyes
were open too in a new way
no longer locking on the object they needed
to look at with a seizure of grasping
but a smiling yet active embrace
of the visible panoply–

horizon, atmosphere, depth, and pulsation
of being   together
                    beneath the
sweep and rapture of a
seeing that
need not gaze …

Set Speaks!

I'll cut you up
  or down
you'll lie down
 in a puddle
  of your own pieces
waiting for the horses
to make a magical pass above the fragments
of your nature   find
  all of them
 however randomly distributed
            among the sundry
  attitudes and thought forms
            that distracted you
these horses fly out from the fingers of the magus as he
adapts himself to his post as
Director of Operations in your mind
did you think it was your own
 intelligence that organized this universe?
 gave direction to each movement of the
   practice and the flows
rising from hidden frozen stuck spots
longtime dead or numb terrain
  the body is the earth
 and whole populations lie in
   mortuary slumber
they don't even know they are waiting for anything
  but every dream
      contains a whistle
  and when the magus blows it
some fragment of your being awakens
 just long enough to flash upon the whole
   from which it long ago had blown away ...

Five Names

Assume the worst. The soul
has five names. Call them.

Call the soul by five
peculiar animals /
images.

A woman
with the head of a viper an-
other with no head. Heads and shoulders above
a third whose right angles
dream
a third order of
derision—

That's one name. The three-fold disturbance
within the monadology of the psychoid. A bleeding—
staunchless, dearthward.
The vitiate world.
The pregnable.

On earth
the earth itself
projected.

That means the soul
is combined
of earthly
originals, earthly kinds
combine
to shake it up
or shake it down. Down and out,

all return
to elements, these
return to that
that pitched them forth. There is nothing
to it but its own
combinatory. When this goes
it is as though
it had never been. No. More than that.
No more than that. It
had never
been.

◆

Another
name's
the moon. What's on the moon? What's
in
a soul. By any other
moon
mere
breath
passes
between us.

But ON the moon, such
words as such
as we exchange
extenuate a universe
of passage, passing ON
words. On the other
side
of the moon, all
words are done.

◆

Sun.
Mind's
force
contracts
intelligence. A small
disease
disturbs, conveys. All space and time so thoroughly
inspirited, commonality so heartily endowed, that
a singular portal, its tariff not unpaid, appears
as if
therein. But there is no "in." Only
up
and down.

◆

Life
is its own
name. We have been traveling inward
up
AND
down
along an
exigent
carriageway.
The vital chariot
whose walls are flames
whose horses
draft
the mind along
wonted corridors
and avenues of beryl—bliss states
governed by teleologies no mind
convened—*that* chariot.

This chariot itself comprises the other names.
These repeat themselves silently, endlessly,
as the vast wheels turn.

◆

The fifth name names no substance.
The fifth world turns no songs.
There is a point
and
as soon as that word's out
the point recoils
returns
upon its own relief
and opens
homeword to what cannot NOT.
Eleutheria and Anangke, cleave.
No more than that.
No. More than that.
A marriage made in a place
Where all marriage is forgot.
Thalamus and Thelemite.
A king and queen alight on an empty throne.

NOTES

The thinking that *goes in* to a poem or that can be *awakened* as its "further life"[1]—like the fuzzy temporal location of particles in quantum reality—exists more like a cloud than a thing. Do these thoughts precede or succeed their poems? But the poems themselves do not have unique temporal onset: they link on to each other and to the texts and thoughts that environ them, in the problematic temporal topology of textuality itself, appearing after the fact yet in the guise of that which uncovers "meanings" in, of, and from them.

These notes, then, are a "further life," in my own thinking, of the poems themselves. I certainly could not have produced the thought in the poems before I produced the poems—but the notes show the poems to be the "further life" of texts and thoughts that, in a literally "cymatic" sense, have "influenced" them—i.e., flowed *in* them, or flowed them *in*.

theforestforthetrees

Begun in 1982, *theforestforthetrees* was originally a name for my writing in poetry, but it has since proved to contain photographs, drawings, text-sound texts, sound poems and performances, music, philosophy, and miscellaneous prose. I have also recognized work from before the declaration of "the forest" as belonging to it so that now it is a name for all my "creative" activity.

Most importantly *theforestforthetrees* was never the name for a "long poem," but rather comprises the accumulation of unedited writings *as* they accumulated day by day. Culled collections, edited texts, publications, public and private readings, web-postings, are therefore all "from *theforestforthetrees.*"

---

[1] In our collaborative, "dialogical" writings, George Quasha and I frequently use the phrase "the future life of the work" to characterize discourse, art, work, conversation, or any vital experience arising from some work that "furthers" its creative impulse(s).

117

The Hat Rack Tree

My father kept a grand hydrangea bush. It had magnificent plumes in summer, but a scraggly hierarchy of clipped and naked branches out of season. Good for nothing but a rack to hang your hat on, he called the naked bush his "hat rack tree." Like the skeleton of a way of thought, I thought; a (kabbalistic) tree of life that, seeming to assert nothing, serves as a cognitive scaffold, a schema to hang your images on.

◆

Donnings and doffings of often headless hats haunt the *forest*. Hats suffer the fates of the identities they betoken and effectuate. A short poem in *The Hat Rack Tree* reads:

> My hat had vanished.
>
> When that cat that
> sat up looked straight at it,
>
> that hat had had it.

The cat's intensity vanquishes the identity that is the target of its massive concentration. I found the following item among *forest* notes from the early '80s too late for inclusion in *The Hat Rack Tree* volume:

> The forms
> fall off
> the hat rack
> tree.
>
> The hats
> go back
> to the sky.

As the poem strikes me now, there is celebration here of a liberative moment, when the fixities of appearance fall away, and the icons of identity levitate, or the principle of structure, imparted by the tree to that which hangs upon it, exchanges secrets with the indeterminate.

The closing and title poem of *The Hat Rack Tree* turned out to be the first in a series of poems. I repeat its publication here to be true to the sense of that series.

◆

"No wind is the King's Wind" (page 3)

A refrain from Confucius (is it?) in Pound's Canto whatever, primes for me an open inquiry into contingency, randomicity, spontaneity, and the forces of morphogenesis and order.

◆

The demagogue and technologist would put the wind under his hat; while the magus or the Taoist would *ride* the wind.

How High the Moon

The reach of mutability is micrological: exactly when in the mind does the next thought arise? Or when will the nucleus of the uranium atom tunnel its next beta particle?

The sublunary world is the world of change, but under the ontological regime that rules the West from late antiquity until—when shall we put it? Copernicus? Edmund Spencer? Yeats? change itself is thought to fall under a rule: a Wheel of Fortune governs life. One never knows when one's fortune will change or how it will fall; but fortune itself is cyclical, the very paradigm of order. Contemporary "chaos" theory adds only complex ramifications to the paradigm, but the inter-inalienability of aleatory and pattern remains in view.

Against traditional lunar symbolism, this poem wants to know what remains true in mind while momentary thoughts usher in an utterly transitory and unanticipatable world; for the orb of the moon, though subject to change by phases, in its fullness seems also to hold *against* all change. (See "The Hermit" in this volume, page 91.)

In the moment of meditation in March, 1971 when I realized that the context of my spiritual life in fact was Buddhism, I felt with the deepest tentacles of my intellect something like the singular orb of the moon standing alive in empty light, beyond the very cessation of my random ratiocination.

Crow's Head Run

"the order type of the continuum" (page 29)
Also see: *"Now I can do anything ... "* (page 54)

The undifferentiated continuum, one might say, is a primordial intuition that suggestively ingresses in many regions of mathematical, physical, mystical, cosmological, and ontological thinking. Parmenides almost says that Being is One Continuum, and it is precisely its undifferentiable character—that it can neither be distinguished from what *outside it* is *NOT* it, nor subdivided internally—that his disciple Zeno was paradoxically concerned to articulate in his famous paradoxes. Einstein-Minkowsky Space/Time is the Space-Time *Continuum*, and it is this characteristic of the theories of relativity that brings them into conflict with Quantum Theory, the latter being essentially a theory of *dis*continuity. At dispute is whether material reality is modeled by the continuum.

In mathematics, "order type" refers to the hierarchy of infinite magnitudes due to Georg Cantor, the founder of set theory and the originator of the theory of transfinite number. Cantor burned out trying to demonstrate that the "order type" of the continuum is the smallest infinite collection that *cannot* be put into an order measured by the natural numbers. In the 1960s it was demonstrated that Cantor's "continuum hypothesis" is arbitrary and that a set theory can be constructed either on its basis or on its contrary. Indeed, one can have different set theories depending on the choice of *which* infinity, if any, is to be construed as denoting the "power" of the continuum.

The calculus is the study of continua, and, after the work of Dedekind and Cantor, it has the peculiarity of defining the continuum itself in terms of infinite classes of divisions or *cuts*: each number—rational or real—is a discrete division of the continuum. The question of the continuum hypothesis becomes a question of how many ways the continuum—the undivided and indivisible whole—can be divided! Different answers to this question are the different "order types." If the continuum itself is subject to arbitrary variation, the application of the calculus to model the physical universe raises the question referred to in my poem.

For me, the paradox of the infinite divisibility of the indivisible profoundly resonates the primordial question at the root of most traditional cosmogonies, gathered by Heidegger in his question about "Ontological Difference" and generalized succinctly by G. Spencer Brown in his Calculus of Indications. How can undifferentiated and indeterminate Being proliferate the multiplicity of articulated beings?

Something From An Outside

There is no single "outside"—only singular outsides—whose incursions within conventional reality are paradoxical, unassimilable; yet the "potential" awakened by their difference from all we take to be real marks the boundary of an "ontological set" and restores a dynamic polarity to apparent being that normality holds in flaccid depotentiation. (See "The Hermit" in this volume, page 91.)

The aliens with their almond-eyes, as image, might signal this paradox—the sense of an unwitnessed witness—a consciousness whose ontological dimensions cannot be assessed; whose interactions with us can neither be evaded nor conceptually integrated.

According to John Clarke, for the cosmological poet, the incursion of that which is outside the thralldom or closure of one's sense of reality—whether the incursion manifests in dream, meditation, or through social or physical encounters—imparts a charge of creative potential. "Manifests of Momentary Incursion" must be stashed away for later expenditure in the poem.

Unless so-anchored in a work, reality is a dubious enchantment—incursion breaks the spell, but does so by delivering the possibility of enchantment renewed or new enchantment. Fearfully, the transformation or re-charging of one's reality set may appear as a deepening of the reality to which one has always been enthralled. Possibility itself is then but the play of ontological possession—possession by the real or a limited view of the real.

To break the spell, there are Tibetan and other practices requiring long retreats in complete seclusion, silence, and darkness, where awareness finds itself disoriented with respect to night and day, dream and reality, sleep and waking, and the presence and absence of that which appears to appear; for all that appears in the dense vacuity of prolonged optical and auditory deprivation is the creation of one's somatic life and active mind. As this activity settles into quiescence or reveals aspects of its structure, deep layers of one's tendencies to form a world arise and dissolve.

It isn't that we know the statistical character of incursive events: whether they arise from an aleatoric field, proceed along some hidden causal chain, or open fatal intersections between the current narrative of our existence and some transcendent pattern or plan. But at the juncture of their occurrence, they disrupt our ontological order. At the site of disruption, imagination awakens. And what we imagine may conduct a destiny.

The dream in this poem refers to another dream that occurred during such a "dark retreat" in which an identity from another time and life seemed mine, articulating some old familial drama. My father's "blood line" was implicated in a "cult" that *was* a certain "song": its singers or pop fans belonged to it, and the song sang itself to be "the essence of love." This cult had an enemy, and I was to understand that my identity—the deep structure of its boundaries, its conflicts—was shaped by the saga of its cultic struggles.

From Mimir's Head

The title for this section and for this compilation as a whole is taken from a poem by Gerrit Lansing. The poem is "The End of Nature in This World," from his *Heavenly Tree / Soluble Forest*. The relevant lines are:

> boiling from the spring,
> black, spew of Mimir's head,
> murderous astringency

referring perhaps to the alchemical *Nigredo*—the wrathful, *blackening* of alchemical matter, from which all possibilities are germinate.

In the mythology of Northern Europe, Mimir was the severed head of an exceedingly wise being among the Frost Giants, associated with the Aesirs. Mimir was exchanged as a forfeit in the primordial conflict between the two groups of gods, the Aesirs and the Vanirs. When the truce was broken, the Vanirs slew Mimir, but his head was embalmed and magically kept awake. In this state he continued to function as a counselor to Odin, the god of magic. What issues from him is, I say, Possibility itself, articulated as prophetic and poetic utterance.

In other aspects of the myth, Mimir dwelled at the foot of Yggdrasill, the World or Axis Tree, near a miraculous spring, so Yggdrasil is also known as the Tree of Mimi, or Mimir.

One might well think of a severed head as a disembodied intellect—an icon for the mind's loss of its somatic roots and chthonic powers. But Mimir's head is elemental earth and water. Though the subject of primal war and conflict among archetypal potencies, it shows the mind/head as embodied even so. An intelligence that will not be struck from its corporeal context in spite of violent contingency, it sings of possibility imbuing the actual.

The Ogdoad

In Helenistic gnosis, there is an "eighth sphere" or "Ogdoad" beyond the seven associated with the astrologically efficient planets. Having thrown off the domination exerted by the characteristics of these seven spheres, one enters the Ogdoad, the zone proper to oneself; from there the gnostic launches an ascent to deification and final union with Primordial Mind. The poem was written as a sort of "footnote" to my translation of "The Poimandres" from the *Corpus Hermeticum*.

The Sampo

A "Sampo" in the *Kalevala* is a "world frame." My poem works a multi-cultural myth developed by John Clarke in one of the great works of advanced mythopoetic imagination of the century just gone by, *From Feathers to Iron*. [Tombouctou / Convivio, 1987, Bolinas]. Clarke's book is an edited transcription of a series of lectures (with questions from the audience), richly annotated by Clarke himself. Clarke thinks, here, of the poet's work in this way:

> CLARKE: You make a replica of what the *Kalevala* calls a "Sampo." The problem, cosmologically, is that a given Sampo runs down, which you know from the story of Sampson in *Judges*, under the image of his hair being cut and his subsequent loss of strength.... in time he regains his strength and pulls down the pillars of the old world frame.

> AUDIENCE: What's a Sampo?

> CLARKE: *Hamlet's Mill* [Georgio di Santillano] "the setting and the scansion of time." Going back to the original idea of the Flood, you find that the Deluge isn't in the literal meaning of a flood, but is an inundation of a world frame, "water" having to do with the currents of time and so forth. All of a sudden you can see the kind of move the pre-Socratics were attempting to make on Hesiod and Homer: how posit the cosmological ground of mythology so it doesn't simply refer back to a lost Sampo?
> The *Kalevala* poets say that once a given Sampo runs down the only thing to do is make it into a harp, string it and sing songs of sadness at its passing and songs of joy heralding the new: a double-voiced song that looks equally both ways, like Janus.

The Sampo is apparently a mill, the axle of whose mill wheel is the World Axis of Northern European poetry and associated with Yggdrasill. A note to the above text quotes *Hamlet's Mill* (pp. 217-218), in which this mythologem is linked to several others from different ethnic sources:

Proceeding with the labour of felling the miraculous tree, he [the hero Sigu] discovered that the *stump was hollow and full of water.... The water in the cavity,* being *connected with the great reservoir* somewhere in the bowels of the earth, *began to overflow*; and to arrest the rising flood Sigu covered the stump with a *closely woven basket.*

The hero of this tale of the Ackawois of British Guiana has (as Prometheus, Pandora) an earthly counterpart, a "brown *monkey,*" whose

curiosity being aroused by the sight of the basket turned upside down ... imagined that it must conceal something good to eat. So he cautiously lifted it and peeped beneath, and *out poured the flood.*

Something nervous at the end of the line ...

Before the current diaspora of Tibetan teachings and the opening of their secrets to all who wish to know them, the practice kept most secret and regarded with most awe, if consummated, yielded visions of a chain or string of visually accessible spherettes, containing all the possibilities of experience itself. I image these here as a sequentially realized combinatorial matrix, the apprehension of which unblocks an ultimate concern that percolates beyond/within them.

Like pure Parmenidean Being that can neither be experienced phenomenally nor differentiated conceptually, yet adheres like a resin to all that comes to apparency or comes to mind—the enlightened function in the Dzogpa Chenpo tradition in Tibetan Bonpo and Nyingmapa Buddhism outrides the experiences that issue from it. A certain Master, when asked about his experience of enlightenment, pointedly remarked, "I experience nothing."

The term for this enlightened function is frequently translated as "presence" or "presence in the instant," but its work beyond the phenomenal and the conceptual surely suggests a sense of "presence" not clearly folded in the closure of the "metaphysics of presence" so copiously deconstructed in recent philosophy. In fact "presence" here is neither a subject constituted by and correlated with what can become present to it, nor any sort of object that might be so presented. Rather it would be *that for which* what comes to presence might do so, but which is not limited either by what presences or its presencing.

Canto

I have a project in photography concerned with various registrations of light on water. If I ever have the money, I will reproduce a series of these images in a further edition of this book. The photographs belong to the same "region" of the *"forest"* as this group of poems; they were made during the same years, and often at the sites at which any number of the poems were composed—Heart Lake, Harris Lake, and Newcomb Lake in the Adirondacks, various streams in the Catskills; and they issued from states of meditation that they were in fact the extensions of.

My practice was to sit by the side of the water for some time, and, guided by the altered time sense and body sense the meditation opened, set up to photograph the water surface, the fleeting luminous phenomena occurring on it, and whatever objects—mostly stones and leaves—were apparent to the camera lenses through it. The photographic images do seem, as I say, to be the extension of the meditation itself, uncannily suggesting a luminous sentience inhabiting the interior of the body—a world of liquid functions, transposing and registering transitory beings of palpable light.

Recently I read of developments in the physiology of somatic energy wherein the propagation of waves of internal sentience happens as luminous piezoelectric currents along the liquid crystal surface of the fascia—the sheet of connective tissue enfolding all muscles, tendons, organs, and linking the grosser movements of the body to the intricate webwork of tissue and cell.

Phenomenal mind might be an exfoliation of inner light on inner water; a webwork sensitive to our most intimate concerns; and when those concerns in practiced meditation "field" questions of the intimate character of being itself as it unfolds in embodied thought—well, just so.

The Tower

In the Western esoteric system I studied in the early 1960s, the Tarot card called "The Lightning Struck Tower" symbolically encodes the following symbolic nexus: The Tower, built of discrete building blocks, is both the human body with its cellular construction, and human language with its phonemes, morphemes, parts of speech, etc. As the body encodes its own genealogy within its cells, language introjects the social origin of thought through the common nature of linguistic convention and meaning. Language is thus complexly inextricable from embodiment.

In the tradition, the human being inhabits this language/body as a dyadic principle of sentience and energy, a male/female dyad, and comes to build its own body-tower through accumulating self-cognition as mediated by the language at its disposal. In the end one comes to live within the prison-tower of embodied language as trapped energy and conditioned consciousness. But affinity with energy promises release in the form of adventitious dynamic incursions: bolts from the blue—lightning striking, tossing the little people from the tower top, liberating energy and mind.

In *The Hat Rack Tree* a poem called "The Tower" celebrated this myth of cosmically sourced, salutary, if violent eviction. The Tower, here, suggests an inversion of this process.

Extra Notes On The Poetics of The Possible

Gotlob Frege says somewhere that even the most assertive of poems actually asserts nothing. Its formulations may be extracted to express assertions, but that is a different matter. This may seem to enervate the ontological relevance of poetry, yet poetry harbors *the possible* by being the modality of utterance in which being is *suspended* just where it appears to be *asserted*.

◆

Nothing is so, in a final sense, as uttered; but the need to utter our take on what is so is inalienable—we do it all the time in our gestures, our cogitations, our idle talk, the negotiation of our relationships, our dreams. Either all such activity is futile and enclosed within a nature whose reality is forever alien from its motivating desire—or in this very inalienableness, the well-nigh continuous emission of ontological assertiveness nests an authentic link onto being: not that our assertions are true—but that in the actuality of our need to utter them there is an adhesion in/to being that we glance over in our haste to complete our gesture or our discourse.

◆

The philosopher should be discouraged in his metaphysical pretension, but the metaphysician encouraged in his poetic need.

◆

No assertion is uniquely true, but all modalities of assertion link onto truth. In this, poetry, music, theology, speculative philosophy, scientific theory, and deconstructive discourse are in the same boat. Their claims to truth rest on something in their processes that runs on authentic concern. They betray this concern when the need for finality, certainty, authority, or probity overrides their impulse.

◆

Rhyme is speculative analogy—rhyme, that is, in the sense of heard equivalence—wherever it occurs.

A rhyme is a speculation on an identity: a connection is proffered, not asserted. If the conceptual analogy is uncovered by further reflection, this reflection in any case belongs to the mind of the reader. If the analogy is felt nevertheless to be essential to the poem, then it must be said that the reader's subsequent reflection is essential to it too.

Science wishes its analogies to be taken seriously, not speculatively. And scientific thought abounds in analogy. Physics strives to unify diverse phenomena through the articulation of universal laws. Particularly the new sciences of complexity and far-from-equilibrium thermodynamics discover abundant analogies between diverse scales and domains of phenomena. But the bases of such analogies are simply the mathematical structures elicited to describe the phenomena; and if we reflect upon the ontological status of these mathematical descriptions, we find that any determination of such status is in fact speculative, so that the strong contrast between speculative and positive analogy breaks down. Scientific analogy turns out to be rhyme too.

The Hermit

The "outside" appears *within* a ring or rim of fire. It is a flaming portal or porthole through which I am granted momentary access to what does not originate in me or in my time. Breathing seems to stop for a moment, but no, it has not stopped. There it is again; a surge of time has arisen and vanished there where I thought that time itself had ceased to be. Time is both strangely intimate and alien. Inalienable. The engine that drives the core.

The continuity of (in)alien time does not conduct a passage from this moment to that. At every point there is a new, and newly alien, origin of temporal motion. All that would conduct consciousness along a path lies outside the ring: it has already been assimilated to my own projection, fixed even in its seemingly fluid transiency as a factor in the composition of my world. Inside the ring, time has no such program. It will not contribute to a worldly or personal trajectory. The outside (inside) is neither physical externality, nor the impersonal webnet of structural relations. It is the transcendence itself.

From the rim: gaze back upon memory, experience, knowledge, thought, existence. The labyrinthine passageways. Or imagine a figure for whom access to the rim is constant. The poem reads such a figure in the alchemical Artifex and the Hermit of the esoteric tarot. The Lantern Man.

Significant images emerge for poetry neither from within or without the rim, but rather from the occasion of its proximity. No image captures this situation, of course, yet momentary contact, momentary access, momentary incursion, occurs, giving rise to a site where the unimaginable delivers itself up to transitory imaging.

An image seized from the transitory is a perilous thing: it charges itself with an infinite potentiation. It distributes and concentrates power. To retain its charge, it must seal the breach from whose proximity it receives its potency.

No matter. The breach will open again. Time will recommence. The frozen image will dissipate in the event of its own renewal.

Point of Names

I was not consciously exercised by the coming of the new millennium. Therefore it surprised me when this clutch of apocalyptic celebrations presented themselves in the months immediately following Jan 1, 2000. They assimilate fragments of contemporary late-night, ecstatic/paranoiac radio occultism, to which I attribute nothing but what is reflected in these poems.

If we are to enjoin a witch-hunt against all fundamentalisms, we must certainly smoke out the occultists and esotericists when, contrary to their own richest possibilities and the extravagant cognitive permission which they enjoy, they close themselves up in exclusivities and positivities, among which I might list: the literal and exclusive commitment to particular systems of correspondence; too explicitly realized data for the dates of events in Atlantaean history; certainties about the inhabitants of Sirius, Aldebaran, the Pleiades, the invisible 10th (or 12th) solar planet, and God help us, Mars. But mythologies adhered to and expressed with rigor afford a certain stimulus to the imaginal faculty when accompanied by appealing ethical generalities or instructions in contemplative technologies.

Such was the case with a certain esoteric system, in connection with which a bit of writerly drudge work fell my way early in the year 2000, which explains the content of "Pineal Matters," the untitled poem beginning "and sat down" And "Set Speaks."

I am constrained not to disclose the specific system in question, but suffice it to say that I ghost wrote a small volume of cosmic history and this supplied me with the data and moral expectation in these three pieces.

The Point in It

The *Zohar* speaks of the first gesture of ontological emergence
as a point, but a point brings along with it the space in which it
is inscribed, so the final determination of this initial rupture with
the unmanifest, even though it does not in itself go even as far
as prescribing a *first distinction*, nevertheless calls forth from an
indeterminate futurity, all possible dimension.

The point surrounded itself with a palace. It filled the palace with
light, the Zohar says. But one can see the luminous emanation from
a point as a sphere or tigle, in fact the primal tigle, tigle chenpo:
the unexceeded spherical; and that the sphere is a sphere in infinite
dimensions; and that, as I say, it is co-original with its point. There is
both process and preformation here. Expansion without exhaustion,
continuous effluence, but also timeless figuration. Continuum. All the
numbers called in one. All the colors in a single hue. All the sounds
called back beforehand to the first instant (instance) of vocalization.

Thus the eternal freshness of any dawn whatever. As if the entire
itinerary of the diurnal circuit were not infinitely prescribed. What is
a circle anyway, that he should follow her? Our physicists and our
geometers, I fear, have neglected this question.

Pineal Matters

I'm not sure when the pineal body became the focus of esoteric
intervention—whether Descartes' belief that it is the seat of
consciousness started the business, or whether knowledge of its
spiritual function arises more deeply ensconced in traditionary gnosis
or speculation. But by the time I was a student of occultism in the
early 1960s, it was "common knowledge" that spiritual awakening
and, particularly, the "opening of the third eye" depended upon the
pineal gland's recovery of its dormant powers. Until recent times,
exoteric medicine found no use for the thing.

The Five Names

Bad enough that Being assumes the name "Being" (or that "Being" assumes that Being has a name) : the name "Being" is surely one name too many, though, on second thought, it is perhaps the only name about which this can be said.

Here, five names appear—a desperate proliferation. Better go all the way and name all things.

There are presentations of the Kabbalah where the soul has five names, betokening a stacked hierarchy, ascending from somatic elements to a soul root in the folds, processes, and (dis)figurations of the Godhead—snakes and breaths and lights; garments, palaces, nations: transparitions of images. The five names are coupled with the earth, the moon, the sun, the Merkabah Chariot, the Primal Point. Their Hebrew names are Nephesh, Neshamah, Ruach, Chai, and Yechidah. In this poem, the Zoharic imagery for these stages is side-stepped or side-swiped, and a parallel quincunx is allowed to appear.

About the Author

CHARLES STEIN (born 1944 in New York City) is the author of thirteen books of poetry including a new verse translation of *The Odyssey* (North Atlantic Books) and *The Hat Rack Tree,* (Station Hill Press). His prose writings include a vision of the Eleusinian Mysteries, *Persephone Unveiled* (North Atlantic Books), a critical study of the poet Charles Olson's use of the writing of C.G. Jung, *The Secret of the Black Chrysanthemum* (Station Hill Press), and a collaborative study with George Quasha of the work of Gary Hill, *An Art of Limina: Gary Hill's Works & Writings,* Ediciones Poligrafa. He holds a Ph.D. in literature from the University of Connecticut at Storrs and lives with guitarist, choral director, photographer, and research historian, Megan Hastie in Barrytown, New York. His writings and photography can be accessed at www.charlessteinpoet.com.

CPSIA information can be obtained at www.ICGtesting.com
Printed in the USA
BVOW010451281112

306638BV00002B/58/P